I·N·S·I·D·E
SPAIN

Ian James

Franklin Watts
London · New York · Sydney · Toronto

CONTENTS

© 1989 Franklin Watts
96 Leonard Street
London EC2

Published in the USA by
Franklin Watts Inc.
387 Park Avenue South
New York, N.Y. 10016

Franklin Watts Australia
14 Mars Road
Lane Cove
NSW 2066

Design: K & Co
Illustrations: Hayward Art Group

UK ISBN: 0 86313 839 X
US ISBN: 0-531-10834-1
Library of Congress Catalog
Card Number: 89-8873

Phototypeset by Lineage Ltd, Watford
Printed in Belgium

SPAIN

Front cover: ZEFA
Back cover: ZEFA
Frontispiece: Chris Fairclough

Photographs: J Allen Cash 19;
Mary Evans Picture Library 8, 22;
Chris Fairclough 5t, 6, 14, 16t, 16b,
17, 21, 23, 24t, 24b, 25, 26, 27, 29, 30;
Hutchison Library 18; Popperfoto 8;
Rex Features 9, 28; ZEFA 4, 5b, 7,
10, 11t, 11b, 12, 13, 15, 20.

The land

Spain, the third largest country in Europe after the Soviet Union and France, faces the Atlantic Ocean in the north and the Mediterranean Sea in the east and south. It shares with Portugal a block of land called the Iberian peninsula.

Most of Spain consists of a high plateau called the Meseta. Its flat surface is broken by mountain ranges. The highest range is the Sierra Nevada in the southeast. Other ranges include the Galician Mountains in the northwest, the Cantabrian Mountains in north-central Spain, and the Pyrenees, along the border with France. The main lowlands are the Plains of Aragon in the north and the Plains of Andalusia in the south.

Below: **Scenic cliffs and bays with sandy beaches are features of Spain's coastlines.**

Left: **Rugged mountains run across northern Spain from west to east.**

Below: **Much of the Meseta consists of flat plains. Large areas are farmed.**

5

Spain includes the Balearic Islands in the
Mediterranean Sea. This group contains the
tourist islands of Mallorca, Menorca and
Ibiza. Another island group, the volcanic
Canary Islands, lie about 95 km (60 miles)
off the coast of northwest Africa in the
Atlantic Ocean.

Northern Spain has a mild, moist climate.
Forests cover large areas. By contrast, the
mainland Meseta is a dry region, with hot
summers and cold winters. Most of the
forests that once covered the Meseta have
been cut down. Stripped of its natural plant
cover, parts of the Meseta have been turned
into semi-desert. The Mediterranean coasts
and the Balearic Islands have hot, dry
summers and mild, moist winters.

Above: **The dry, but fertile
plains of Andalusia in the
south are the hottest parts
of mainland Spain.**

The people and their history

The country's official language is Castilian Spanish. But about one out of every four people speak other languages, notably Gallego in the northwest, Basque in north-central Spain, and Catalan in the northeast. Regional parliaments have been set up so that people speaking minority languages can have more control over their affairs. Some Basques would like to form their own independent country.

The modern history of Spain began in 1492, when Christian armies took Granada, the last Arab (or Moorish) stronghold in Spain. In the same year, Christopher Columbus discovered for Spain the New World of the Americas.

Below: **The Alhambra, a Moorish stronghold in Granada, fell to Christian armies in 1492. The Moors had ruled much of Spain from the 8th century.**

Above: **The defeat of the Armada (the Spanish fleet) in 1588 and the loss of half of its ships began a gradual decline of Spain as a major world power.**

Right: **General Francisco Franco ruled Spain from 1939 to 1975. He restored peace after the civil war, but at the expense of civil liberties.**

Spain was a great world power in the early 16th century. But a series of wars slowly weakened Spain. It lost most of its empire and, by the early 20th century, it had become a poor farming country.

Its people were divided. Some wanted Spain to continue as a monarchy. Others wanted it to become a republic. A civil war began in 1936. When it ended in 1939, Spain became a dictatorship headed by General Francisco Franco. Franco died in 1975 and Spain again became a monarchy. King Juan Carlos I became Head of State, and the country is ruled by an elected government and parliament. In 1986 it joined the European Economic Community.

Below: **A political rally in Madrid in 1986. Spain became a parliamentary democracy under a new Constitution introduced in 1978.**

Towns and cities

In recent years, many people have moved from the countryside into the towns and cities. Between 1930 and 1985, the proportion of people in the countryside fell from 75 to 23 per cent. In the north, the land is divided into small farms. The farming population there is widely scattered. But much of central and southern Spain is divided into large estates and farmworkers live in villages or towns.

Many towns and cities are old. The Phoenicians founded Cádiz and Málaga nearly 3,000 years ago. The Carthaginians founded Barcelona in about 230 BC. Six cities have more than 500,000 people. They are Madrid, the capital, Barcelona, Valencia, Seville, Zaragoza and Málaga.

Below: **The village of Pobla de Segur is on a river which flows swiftly down the south slopes of the Pyrenees mountain chain.**

Left: **Behind the port of Barcelona is a famous tree-lined avenue called the Ramblas. It contains bookstalls, pet shops, flowerstalls and open-air restaurants.**

Right: **Central Valencia contains many historic medieval and Renaissance buildings.**

Madrid lies in central Spain on the Meseta, about 655 m (2,150 ft) above sea level. It stands on the site of a Moorish fortress, built more than 900 years ago. It became important in 1561, when King Philip II made it the capital.

Madrid is the second most important industrial city after Barcelona. Because of its many industries, Madrid suffers from pollution and congestion. But central Madrid remains an elegant place, with pleasant avenues, parks and fine buildings. It is the home of the royal family and it contains one of the world's greatest art galleries, the Prado. This gallery contains many great paintings by such artists as El Greco, Francisco Goya and Diego Velázquez.

Above: **The Royal Palace in Madrid is used by the King to entertain foreign visitors. The King lives in Zarzuela Palace near Madrid.**

Family life

Family ties in Spain are close. Most young people live with their parents. The mother is the central member of the family. Young women were, until recently, kept under strict control until they married. But today, girls have much more freedom.

Most country people live in small houses, but most city people live in apartments. In the hotter parts of Spain, everyone, including children, goes to bed later than in most of Western Europe. This is because people take a siesta, or nap, after lunch, and work until 8 p.m. or later. In the evening, the family does not eat until 10 or 11 p.m. Some people believe that they should end this system.

Below: **Many people live in farming villages made up of small, white-washed houses in the central Meseta region.**

Left: **Tall apartment buildings house many people in the northern city of Bilbao in the Basque Region.**

Below: **Television watching is a popular family activity in Spain.**

Food

Shopping hours are from 9 a.m. to 1 p.m. and from 4 to 8 p.m. or later and food shops are open every day. Because Spain is a hot country, fish, fruit and vegetables are major foods.

Breakfast usually consists of coffee or hot chocolate, with croissants, toast, or *churros* (deep-fried strips of dough). Lunch, the main meal of the day, is often made up of four courses, such as a soup or omelette, a fish course, a meat dish, and a dessert. People often drink wine with their lunch. When children get home from school, they have a light meal, with pastries or cakes. The late evening meal is often a cold snack, with cold meats, cheese and bread.

Below: **Locally grown fruit and vegetables are sold in this shop on the Mediterranean island of Mallorca.**

The style of cooking varies from region to region. Eastern Spain is famous for *paella*, a meal made from rice, seafood, meat and other ingredients and cooked in an iron pan.

Southern Spain is known for its *gazpacho*, a cold soup made from liquefied vegetables, and its grilled and fried fish dishes. Northern Spain is also known for its fish, especially cod and hake and for *fabada*, a stew which contains sausages and beans. Central Spain is known for its roasts.

Coffee is the chief hot drink, while a popular soft drink, *horchata*, is made from tiger-nuts. Another drink, *sangría*, is made from wine mixed with soda water, ice and fruit.

Below: **Many restaurants in southern Spain have tables in the open air.**

Sports and pastimes

The Spaniards enjoy a wide range of sports, including fishing, golf, skiing, swimming and tennis. The world's fastest ball game, *pelota vasca* or *jai alai*, comes from the Basque region. It is played in a walled court with the bare hand or a basketwork scoop.

The leading spectator sport is soccer. The season runs from September to May and most first class matches are played on Sundays. Several clubs, including Barcelona and Real Madrid, have won international fame. Bullfighting is the most ancient spectacle and most cities have at least one bullring. In 1985, bullfighting attracted 36.1 million spectators, though an increasing number of Spaniards are opposed to bullfighting.

Above: **Pelota is a fast ball game which uses a basketwork catching and throwing device.**

19

Most families once enjoyed a stroll before supper or they talked to their friends and relations in a local square or restaurant. But many people now prefer to stay at home in the evening and watch television.

Most people are Roman Catholics and religious holidays, such as Easter Week, and fiestas celebrating the local saints are occasions which everyone enjoys. People often decorate the streets, dress up in traditional costumes, and organize parades and firework displays. Folk music, singing and dancing are other popular activities during fiestas. Most Spaniards spend their annual vacations at one of the country's many beach resorts.

Below: **Benidorm, north of Alicante, is one of the well known resorts on the Mediterranean Sea.**

The arts

Left: **The Church of the Sagrada Familia in Barcelona is the work of the Catalan architect Antonio Gaudí.**

Spain was once the meeting place of two cultures: Christian and Moorish. Both have left their mark in fine old churches, castles, and Moorish *alcazares* (fortified palaces). The best known Moorish palace is the Alhambra in Granada. The best known modern architect, Antonio Gaudí, designed the unusual and still incomplete Church of the Sagrada Familia in Barcelona.

Great painters include El Greco, a Cretan who painted many masterpieces in Toledo; Diego Velázquez, a court portrait painter and Francisco Goya, who painted scenes from Spanish life and wars. Modern painters include Pablo Picasso, whose cubist paintings are world famous, and the surrealist, Salvador Dali.

21

Spain's best known writer is Miguel de Cervantes, whose comic novel *Don Quixote* was published in the early 1600s. It is one of the greatest works of world literature. Living at the same time as Cervantes were two major dramatists, Pedro Calderón de la Barca and Lope de Vega. The best known modern dramatist is Federico Garciá Lorca.

Spanish folk music and dance, including flamenco, have become world famous. The country's best known composer, Manuel de Falla, wrote an exciting ballet, *The Three-Cornered Hat* in 1919. Spain's most distinguished film-maker was Luis Buñuel, whose first two movies were made with the painter Salvador Dali.

Below: **Don Quixote and his faithful servant Sancho Panza are among the most famous of all characters created by a writer.**

Farming

Until recently, Spain was a mainly farming country. But by 1986, farming employed only 16 per cent of the workforce, as compared with 34 per cent in 1965. Today, most people work in manufacturing and service industries.

Spain remains one of Western Europe's leading food producers. Farmland covers 41 per cent of Spain, pasture 21 per cent, and forests, mainly in the north, 31 per cent.The leading grains are barley and wheat. Apples and pears are grown in the wetter north and citrus fruits and olives are leading crops in the sunny south. Sheep are the leading farm animals, followed by cattle, goats and poultry. Fishing is important.

Below: **Wheat is grown on the Plains of Aragon and on the central Meseta.**

Left: **Grapes for wine-making are grown in vineyards in the sunny region south of Valencia.**

Below: **Fishermen land their catch at Castro Urdiales, a small fishing port near Bilbao, on the north coast of Spain.**

Industry

Spain is generally poor in natural resources. It produces coal, iron ore, and a little oil, but it has to import most of the oil it needs, together with most other raw materials. About half of Spain's electricity is produced at fuel-burning stations. Hydroelectric and nuclear power stations produce the rest.

Before the 1950s, Spain produced various manufactures, including processed food and wines, chemicals, cotton and wool textiles, fertilizers and footwear. Since the 1950s, many new industries have been set up. They include the manufacture of such things as domestic appliances, machine tools, ships, steel and vehicles. Today, Spain is the world's seventh largest car producer.

Below: **A hydroelectric power station in the Pyrenees in northern Spain.**

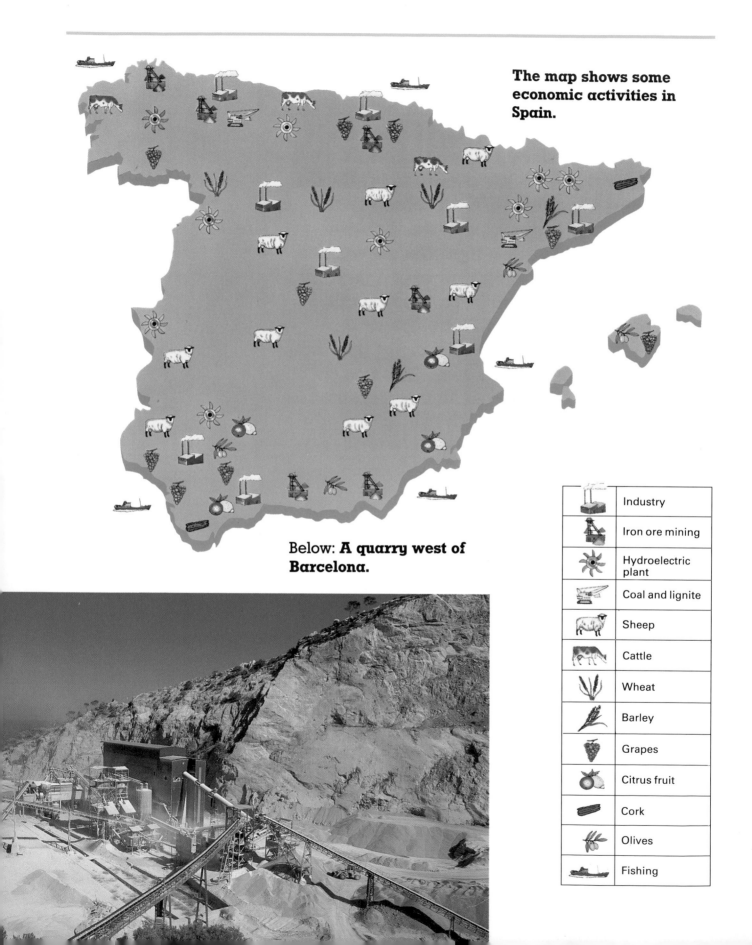

The map shows some economic activities in Spain.

Below: **A quarry west of Barcelona.**

	Industry
	Iron ore mining
	Hydroelectric plant
	Coal and lignite
	Sheep
	Cattle
	Wheat
	Barley
	Grapes
	Citrus fruit
	Cork
	Olives
	Fishing

In the 1980s, Spain set up many new electronics and other high technology industries. Some are backed by foreign companies. For example, in the mid-1980s, a joint United States-Spanish enterprise began to set up Western Europe's biggest microchip factory near Madrid.

The leading service industry in Spain is tourism, which employs about one out of every ten workers. Tourism was almost non-existent in 1950. But by the mid-1980s, the number of tourists going to Spain every year exceeded 40 million. Tourism has provided much needed foreign capital which Spain has used to buy vital imports and to improve services, such as health care and education, which benefit everyone.

Above: **A petrochemical plant in southern Spain makes various products from imported oil.**

Looking to the future

The death in 1975 of the military leader General Francisco Franco ended 36 years of dictatorship. Spain is now a democracy, with complete freedom of speech. its King, Juan Carlos I, is a great supporter of democracy. He has used his influence to persuade military leaders, who do not like change, to remain loyal.

Spain used to be a deeply divided nation. But the rapid rise in living standards has weakened support for extremist groups. Spanish society, especially in the towns and cities, is also changing. One important change concerns young people, especially girls, who have far more freedom and chances for education than their parents.

Below: **King Juan Carlos I and his wife, Queen Sophia, were greeted by the Prince and Princess of Wales on a visit to Britain.**

Spain is changing quickly. But some changes have caused problems. For example, Spain joined the 12-member European Economic Community (EEC) in 1986, because its industries wanted to be able to sell their products in the other countries. But membership of the EEC has increased competition. Old, inefficient industries are disappearing and unemployment has soared.

Some people who speak minority languages still want a greater degree of independence. But in the 1980s, support for extremist groups has decreased, partly because of the setting up of regional parliaments.

Below: **Young people in Spain live in a fast changing country. Many opportunities lie ahead.**

Facts about Spain

Area:
504,782 sq km
(194,897 sq miles)

Population: 39,001,000
(1987)

Capital: Madrid

Largest cities:
Madrid (pop 3,188,000)
Barcelona (1,755,000)
Valencia (752,000)
Seville (654,000)
Zaragoza (591,000)
Málaga (503,000)
Bilbao (433,000)

Official language:
Spanish

Religion:
Christianity

Main exports:
Vehicles and parts,
petroleum products,
fruit and nuts, iron and
steel, footwear and
vegetables.

Unit of currency:
Peseta

Spain compared with other countries

Spain 76 per sq.km.

Britain 231 per sq.km.

USA 26 per sq.km.

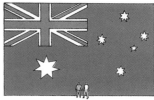

Australia 2 per sq.km.

Above: **Spain is more densely populated than the United States, but less populated than Britain.**

Below: **Spain is much smaller than the United States, but it is the third largest country in Europe.**

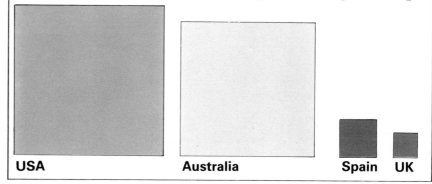

USA **Australia** **Spain** **UK**

Below: **Some of the money and stamps used in Spain.**

Index

Consultant Dr Dennis Ogden
Managing Editor Belinda Hollyer
Editor Bridget Daly
Design Jerry Watkiss
　　　　Sally Boothroyd
Picture Research Susanne Williams
Production Rosemary Bishop
Illustrations Ron Hayward Associates
　　　　John Shackell
　　　　Marilyn Day
　　　　John Mousdale
　　　　Tony Payne
　　　　Raymond Turvey
Maps Matthews & Taylor Associates
　　　　(pages 44–45)

The endpaper picture shows the gold cupolas
of Kremlin Cathedrals

Page 6 shows a parade in Red Square, Moscow

Photographic Sources
BBC Hulton Picture Library 19(TL), 26–7(T),
27(BR). BBC Photographs 23(TR), 32(TR).
Bridgeman Art Library: Marc Chagall, *Les
Mariés*, © ADAGP. Robert Harding Picture
Library 11, 31(T), 38. Courtesy of Kestrel
Books Ltd. 24, 25. Mansell Collection 15(BL),
16(TL). John Massey Stewart 16(R), 33(B).
Dennis Moore 13(L), 17(BL), 30, 31(BL),
34(T)&(B), 34–5, 36, 37(BL)&(TR), 40(TL).
National Palace Museum, Taipei,
Taiwan/BPCC/Aldus Archive 12. Novosti
Press Agency 6–7, 13(R), 14(T), 17(TL),
19(TR), 20–1(B), 22–3(T), 26(BR), 28–9,
29(L), 32(TL), 35(B), 39(B), 41(TR). Hugh
Olliff 10(BL). Rencontre 10(BR), 18(T),
19(BR). Rex Features 21(TR), 33(T). Servizio
Editoriale Fotographico 14(B), 16(BL),
17(TR). Society for Cultural Relations with
the USSR 11, 15(TR), 19(BL), 20(TL), 21(BR),
22–3(B), 26(BL), 27(TR)&(BL). Spectrum
front cover. Frank Spooner Pictures 23(BR),
28(B). Survival Anglia/, Jack Lentfer 8. TASS
28(T), 29(R), 39(TL)&(TR), 41(BR). VAAP
9(T). David Williamson 9(B), 10(T), 11. Bryan
Woodriff 32(B). ZEFA 20–1(T), 31(BR),
40–1(T)&(B).

A MACDONALD BOOK
© Macdonald & Co (Publishers) Ltd 1975,
1986

First published in Great Britain in 1975 by
Macdonald Educational Ltd

This revised edition published in 1986 by
Macdonald & Co (Publishers) Ltd
London & Sydney
A BPCC plc company

Printed and bound in Great Britain by
Purnell Book Production Ltd

Macdonald & Co (Publishers) Ltd
Greater London House
Hampstead Road
London NW1 7QX

British Library Cataloguing in Publication Data

Riordan, James
　　Soviet Union, —2nd ed.—
　　(Macdonald countries)
　　1. Soviet Union—Social life and customs
　　—1970 –
　　I. Title
　　947.085′4　　DK287

ISBN 0-356-11530-5
ISBN 0-356-11531-3 Pbk